THE EGYPTIAN SCIENCE GAZETTE

Where the News Is Ancient History

Laura Layton Strom

children's press®

An imprint of Scholastic Inc.

NEW YORK • TORONTO • LONDON • AUCKLAND • SYDNEY
MEXICO CITY • NEW DELHI • HONG KONG
DANBURY, CONNECTICUT

Library of Congress Cataloging-in-Publication Data

Strom, Laura Layton.
  The Egyptian science gazette / by Laura Layton Strom.
    p. cm. -- (Shockwave)
  Includes index.
  ISBN-10: 0-531-17582-0 (lib. bdg.)
  ISBN-13: 978-0-531-17582-8 (lib. bdg.)
  ISBN-10: 0-531-18813-2 (pbk.)
  ISBN-13: 978-0-531-18813-2 (pbk.)
1. Mummies--Egypt--Juvenile literature. 2. Pyramids--Egypt--Design
and construction--Juvenile literature. 3. Egypt--Antiquities--Juvenile
literature. 4. Science--Egypt--History--To 1500--Juvenile literature.
I. Title. II. Series.

  DT62.M7S84 2007
  932--dc22

2007008942

Published in 2008 by Children's Press, an imprint of Scholastic Inc.,
557 Broadway, New York, New York 10012
www.scholastic.com

08 09 10 11 12 13 14 15 16 17
10 9 8 7 6 5 4 3 2 1

Printed in China through Colorcraft Ltd., Hong Kong

Author: Laura Layton Strom
Educational Consultant: Ian Morrison
Editor: Janine Scott
Designers: Avon Willis and Matthew Alexander
Photo Researchers: Sarah Matthewson and Jamshed Mistry

Photographs by: Aapimage.com: AFP (p. 9); AP (p. 11); © **Kenneth Garrett/
National Geographic Image Collection** (p. 8); **Ingram Image Library** (p. 3);
Jennifer and Brian Lupton (teenagers, pp. 30–31); **John Kingston** (p. 17); **Photodisc**
(King Tut, cover; p. 1); **Photolibrary** (pp. 6–7; dung beetle, p. 19; pp. 23–24; p. 29);
Steve Clarke (p. 16); **TopFoto/www.stockcentral.co.nz** (scarab bracelet, p. 19;
p. 20; p. 27); **Tranz/Corbis** (Ankhesenamun, Horemheb, Ay, cover; p. 5; p. 10;
pp. 12–13; p. 15; p. 21–22; p. 26; p. 28; Rosetta Stone, pp. 30–31)

All illustrations and other photographs © Weldon Owen Education Inc.

CONTENTS

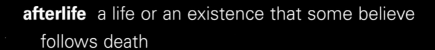

afterlife a life or an existence that some believe follows death

archaeologist (*ar kee OL uh jist*) a scientist who studies people and objects from the past

Egyptologist (*Ee jipt OL uh jist*) an archaeologist who studies ancient Egypt

hereditary (*her ED i tayr ee*) passed from parent to child

hieroglyphics (*hy roh GLI fix*) a system of pictures and symbols that stand for sounds, words, or ideas

mummy a dead body that has been preserved

paleopathology (*pay lee oh puh THAHL uh jee*) the study of diseases of ancient times

pharaoh (*FAIR oh*) a ruler of ancient Egypt

· ·

For easy reference, see Wordmark on back flap.
For additional vocabulary, see Glossary on page 32.

In the word *paleopathology*, *paleo* means "something old or ancient," and *pathology* is "the study of illness or disease." Other examples of words beginning with *paleo* are *paleography*, which means "the study of ancient writing," and *paleontology*, which means "the study of life on earth in earlier times."

Ancient sculpture
of Queen Nefertiti
(ruled 1367–1350 B.C.)

Ancient Egypt fascinates many people. How did ancient Egyptians build **pyramids** without modern machines? Why did they make **mummies**? Who was King Tutankhamen? How did he die?

Much of what we know about ancient Egypt was discovered by scientists. They uncovered **tombs** and temples buried under the desert sand. The dry sand had protected many monuments from robbers. Being buried away from strong sunlight had protected the pictures painted on the walls. Their colors had not faded.

From these discoveries, we have learned much about how the ancient Egyptians lived. Their pictures tell us of their beliefs. The pictures also tell us about the science used by the ancient Egyptians. Now modern science is helping us better understand some of the finds.

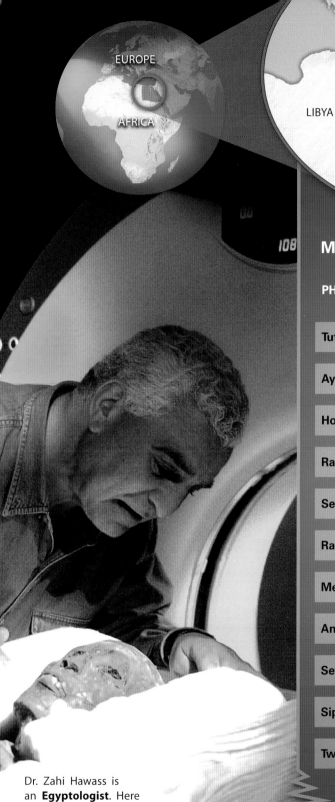

EUROPE

AFRICA

Mediterranean Sea

Giza •• Cairo

LIBYA

EGYPT

Nile River

SAUDI
ARABIA

Valley of the Kings •• Karnak

Red
Sea

AFRICA

MUMMIES OF SOME PHARAOHS

PHARAOH	DEATH DATE	MUMMY FOUND
Tutankhamen	1339 B.C.	1922
Ay	1321 B.C.	not found
Horemheb	1293 B.C.	not found
Ramses I	1291 B.C.	not found
Seti I	1278 B.C.	1881
Ramses II	1212 B.C.	1881
Merneptah	1202 B.C.	1898
Amenmeses	1199 B.C.	not found
Seti II	1193 B.C.	1898
Siptah	1187 B.C.	1898
Twosre (Queen)	1185 B.C.	not found

Dr. Zahi Hawass is
an **Egyptologist**. Here
he studies the mummy
of King Tutankhamen
before it has a **CT scan**.

King Tut murdered?

X-rays used to solve Tut mysteries

by Akila Amenemhet • Senior staff reporter

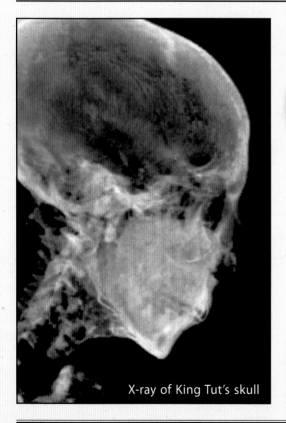

X-ray of King Tut's skull

This headline really helps. It tells me that these pages will be about using X-rays to discover if King Tut was murdered.

The X-ray showed an image of a skull. The doctor pointed to a dark spot on the skull. He nodded his head. "This shows a blow to the back of the head," he said. "This person may have been murdered."

The skull in the X-ray was of a teenage boy. The boy was King Tutankhamen. He was a **pharaoh** who died 3,000 years ago in Egypt.

An X-ray is a photograph of the inside of the body. X-rays can show bones. They can also show some tissues, such as the lungs.

Today, mummies are not unwrapped. They are X-rayed or CT-scanned. But in 1922, when King Tut was found, his mummy was unwrapped. His bones were handled.

Radiologists recently scanned King Tut's body with a CT-scanner. They believe that he may have died from an infection from a badly broken leg. They believe it may not have been from a blow to the head. Did he break his leg in battle? Did he have a **chariot** crash? Was the leg damaged when Tut's mummy was first unwrapped? No one can be sure.

SHOCKER

The CT scan of King Tut was taken in 2005. The scan took 15 minutes. It produced 17,000 images. From these images, we know details about King Tut's health. For instance, he had an impacted wisdom tooth.

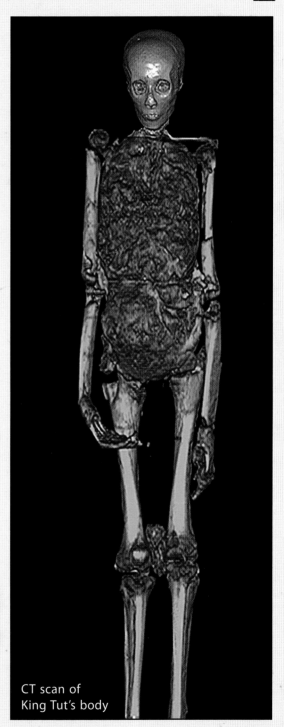

CT scan of King Tut's body

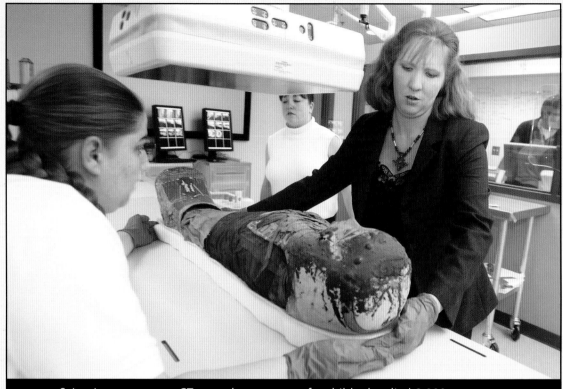

Scientists prepare to CT scan the mummy of a child who died 2,000 years ago.

Mummy doctors to the rescue

by Nathifa Hatshepsut
Medical reporter

It is not every day that scientists invent a new science. The scientific study of mummies has led to a new science called **paleopathology**. It is the study of diseases of ancient times.

Mummies were first found in the 1800s. **Archaeologists** had to unwrap mummies to study them. Sometimes the skeletons were damaged. Today, mummies are studied without unwrapping. Scans of mummies can reveal evidence of diseases. There are remains of **smallpox** scars. Deformed legs can suggest **polio**.

What did King Tut look like?

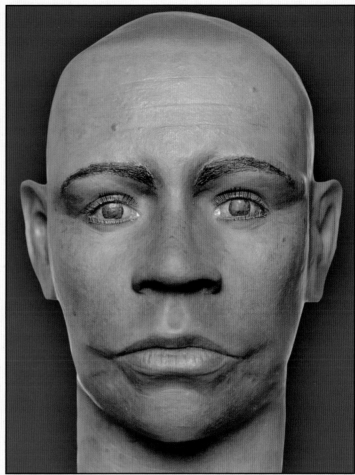

by Nathifa Hatshepsut
Medical reporter

A mummy skull and CT scans have produced the first 3-D model of King Tut's face.

Scientists and artists gathered from Egypt, France, and the United States. They studied 1,700 CT scans. For accuracy, the experts split into three teams. Each team came up with its own model. Surprisingly, all the models of Tut looked similar.

Each model shows Tut to be about nineteen years old. He has the long face seen in his **portraits**. Tut's unusual facial features are similar to some of his **ancestors'** portraits. These shared features suggest that Tut and his family may have shared a **hereditary** secret.

For more on the hereditary secret, see the article on page 22.

Journalists ask students:
"Who Murdered King Tut?"

by Walidah Ranefer • Egypt High School correspondent

The Egyptian Science Gazette is holding a contest for students aged eight to eighteen. The contestants must write a one-page essay. They must state who they think murdered King Tut.

See **Key Suspects** on page 13

King Tut and his wife, Queen Ankhesenamun

Key Suspects

Tut's Prime Minister: Ay ▶

Ay

1. Ay married Tut's wife after Tut died. This made Ay the next pharaoh.

2. Egyptologists found an unusual scene painted in Ay's tomb. It appeared to be that of a murder. People wonder whether Ay was apologizing to the gods for killing Tut.

Ankhesenamun

◀ Tut's wife: Ankhesenamun

1. Ankhesenamun might have believed she would become pharaoh when Tut died.

2. After she married Ay, she is never mentioned again in historical records. People wonder whether she wanted to disappear.

Tut's Military Commander-in-Chief: ▶ Horemheb

Horemheb

1. Horemheb became a pharaoh after Ay. Some people think he wanted the throne. They think that he killed Tut.

2. As pharaoh, Horemheb is believed to have erased all history of King Tut. People wonder whether he was trying to erase his crime by erasing Tut.

Egyptians get their "mummy's" worth

by Zuka Menkaure • Antiquities reporter

Canopic jars

Ebe Fante studies ancient mummies. "Ancient Egyptians believed they needed their bodies in the **afterlife**. Mummy making was an exact science. You needed the right timing, tools, and techniques. It was easy to ruin a mummy," said Fante. The process of making a mummy took 70 days.

First the body organs were removed. The organs were placed in four special containers. These were called **canopic jars**. The body was washed with palm wine. It was also washed with water from the Nile River. This took 15 days. Next the body was packed with salt. It was left to dry for 40 days.

Then the body was stuffed with sawdust or sand. This gave it shape. The body was wrapped in layers of linen. **Amulets** were placed between the layers. The mummy was then sealed in its case.

"Many temples had rooms for making mummies," said Fante. Instructions for mummy making were written in **hieroglyphics** on the walls.

SHOCKER

Many mummies were found in the 1800s. They became so common that people used mummy body parts to decorate their homes.

Wall painting that shows mummy makers preparing the dead

Egyptian Addition

by Mohammed Sudat • Business reporter

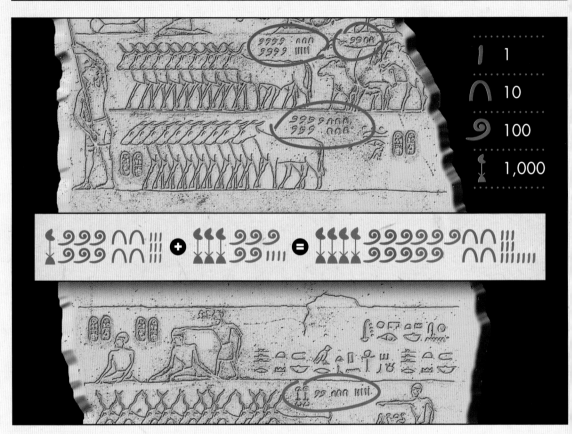

A ncient Egyptians paid taxes, just as people in modern societies do. However, the system of taxing was different. Every year, an official count of animals was held. People then paid taxes to the pharaoh based on the number of animals they owned. They paid in animals or grain. Addition was the basis of much of the mathematics of ancient Egypt. Wall paintings show us that Egyptians had hieroglyphs for numbers. They combined all of the ones, tens, hundreds, and so on. Records were kept to show how many animals a person had.

Many words in the English language can be used as both nouns and verbs. Some examples from this page are: *plant*, *harvest*, *flood*, and *feed*.

Part of a star calendar in an Egyptian tomb

Farmers focus on flashes

by Nut Nefertiti • Astronomy editor

The early Egyptians paid much attention to movements in the planets and stars. The stars helped them decide when to plant. The stars also helped them decide when to harvest crops.

The Egyptians based their calendar on the stars. Sirius was called the Dog Star. When it rose in the night sky, they knew the Nile would soon flood. The annual floods fed the soil. This allowed the Egyptians to grow crops to feed themselves and their animals.

Dung beetles: science or fashion?

by Dr. Umi Narmer
Ancient medicine researcher

The Egyptians believed that small stone objects, called amulets, were powerful charms. They protected the owner from disease and disaster. Instead of medicine, an ancient Egyptian doctor might have given his patient an amulet.

The scarab (*SKAIR ub*) was the most important amulet in ancient Egypt. It was a beetle-shaped charm. Most scarabs were modeled after the Egyptian dung beetle. (*Dung* is another word for *manure*.) A scarab's underside often had a pharaoh's name on it. Some also had important sayings or religious symbols.

The fish amulet in the girl's braid was to protect her from drowning. The amulet at her neck protected her from household dangers.

The dung beetle was considered a lucky creature. The Egyptians thought the beetles grew out of the actual dung. In fact, the beetles rolled dung into pellets. They laid their eggs in the pellets. Dung beetles were a symbol of rebirth or new life.

King Tut's scarab bracelet

Dung beetle

I get it! An amulet is a lucky charm, like a four-leaf clover or a horseshoe. I can often use what I already know to figure out new words.

Scientists piece together history mystery

by Anum Pepi • Computer scientist

Karnak Temple

Scientists in Egypt have solved a 40,000-piece puzzle. It took them six years!

At Karnak Temple in Thebes, the giant temple pillars lay in a crumbled pile. The pieces were **inscribed** with a royal name. The name was that of King Amenhotep IV. Later, the king renamed himself King Akhenaten. Some pieces showed members of the king's family too.

The whole family had very long faces. They also had very narrow eyes.

To read the whole story, Egyptologists had to put the stone drawings together. However, there were 40,000 pieces to arrange.

In 1926, Henri Chevrier tried to put them together by hand. He wanted to rebuild the temple. But too many pieces were missing.

- Scientists wanted to figure out how 40,000 pieces of pillar went together.
- An attempt was made to do this by hand. It failed.
- Finally, photographs and a computer were used.
- Scientists could now solve the mystery.

This shows King Akhenaten with his wife Queen Nefertiti and their children. King Akhenaten was King Tut's father. A different wife, Kiya, was Tut's mother.

Then, in 1965, an American named Ray Winfield Smith had an idea. He had each piece photographed. Later, each photo was fed into a computer. A computer program sorted the pieces. This allowed artists to draw the temple. Then Egyptologists could restore the actual temple. They could also figure out some of the stories.

So why did the king's family have such odd features? Go to the story on page 22. Learn how some scientists believe they have solved this mystery.

King Akhenaten
and Marfan's syndrome

by Kesi Tetisheri • Genetics reporter

Some Egyptian royals had long fingers, long toes, long faces, and narrow eyes. These are some of the features of people with Marfan's **syndrome**.

King Akhenaten was originally named Amenhotep IV. He was pictured at Karnak Temple with these body features. Oddly, so were some of his children. What caused their unusual appearance? Was it hereditary?

Genetic scientists study genes. The genes inside our cells give us our appearance. Sometimes things can go wrong with one of our 25,000 genes. This results in a disorder.

Some scientists believe that Akhenaten's family may have had a genetic disorder. The disorder was Marfan's syndrome. This syndrome causes the physical features seen in the king's family pictures.

One scientist met with a group of modern-day people with Marfan's syndrome. He wanted to get opinions on this idea. When the group looked at pictures of Akhenaten, they gasped. They all believed they were looking at an ancient king with their same disorder.

Scientists don't know for sure that Akhenaten's family had Marfan's. Yet the shared physical features make it likely. Maybe someday a new scientific method will make scientists more sure.

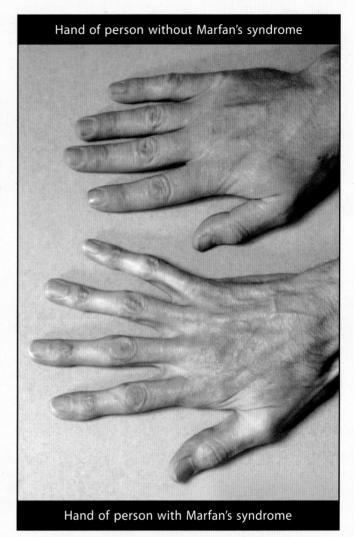

Hand of person without Marfan's syndrome

Hand of person with Marfan's syndrome

At first I couldn't figure out what *syndrome* meant. So I reread the first paragraph and figured out that a syndrome must be a collection of symptoms. Rereading often helps me understand difficult words.

Aliens or clever workers?

by Salih Senwosret • City editor

The Great Pyramid of Giza is the sole survivor of the seven ancient wonders of the world. It is the largest of a group of three pyramids. Many theories have been put forth as to how these monuments were built. Some people even say that the pyramids were built by aliens! Most Egyptologists believe that **canals**, ramps, and shadoofs were used in the construction. Science and mathematics were used to work out a pyramid's **dimensions**. For example, the Great Pyramid's base is almost a perfect square. Its entrance faces true north. The outside stones fit snugly together. A hair cannot be pushed between them.

Shadoof
A shadoof is a tool made with a bucket and a weight. The ancient Egyptians used shadoofs to raise water from the Nile River.

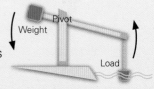

Pyramid Blocks

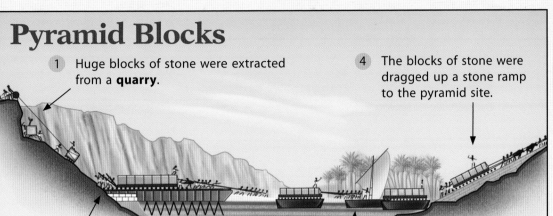

1. Huge blocks of stone were extracted from a **quarry**.

4. The blocks of stone were dragged up a stone ramp to the pyramid site.

2. The blocks of stone were loaded onto **barges**. The barges were floated downriver to Giza.

3. A canal from the river brought the barges to the site.

Pyramid Building

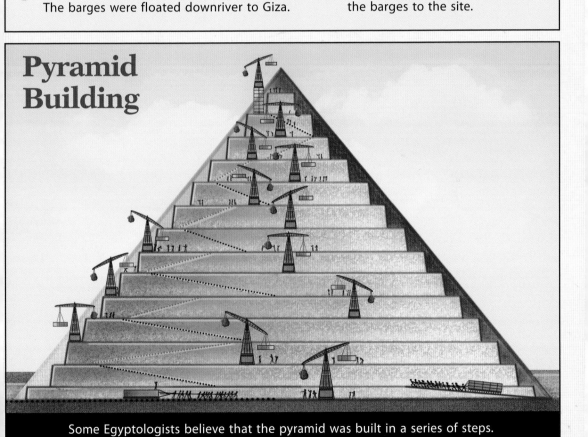

Some Egyptologists believe that the pyramid was built in a series of steps. Sets of shadoofs raised the blocks of stone from one level to the next.

Egyptians punished for a "heavy" heart

by Dr. Kamuzu Tuthmosis • Medical reporter

Love, fear, sadness, and happiness are **emotions**. The ancient Egyptians believed the source of these emotions was the heart. They also believed a person's soul was located in the heart. The heart was the source of life.

The people believed that after death the dead went to a place of final judgment. There the heart of the dead was weighed on a scale. Heavy hearts were said to be loaded down with bad deeds. People with heavy hearts were punished. Those with light hearts were said to have lived a good, honest life. The lighthearted were rewarded. They were sent on to the afterlife.

Today, the words *heartbroken*, *heartache*, and *heavyhearted* describe emotions of sadness and grief. When people say they feel lighthearted, they mean they feel happy and carefree. The Egyptians weren't alone in thinking that emotions come from the heart!

SHOCKER

Some cultures adopted the practice of preserving royal hearts. In the nineteenth century, the Dean of Westminster, in England, bought the heart of King Louis XIV. He ate it!

Weighing the dead person's heart against a feather showed how "heavy" the heart was with misdeeds!

Today, science tells us that our brains are the source of our emotions. Yet a form of the ancient Egyptian belief has settled into our culture. Our language, poetry, and songs tell of broken hearts, for example. Hearts are a symbol of love. It is unlikely that anyone ever sent a valentine in the shape of a brain! Sometimes science and popular culture are at odds with one another.

The Great Sphinx at Giza, Egypt

Egyptologist likes his life with the dead

by Dr. Khai Ramses • Museum curator

Dr. Zahi Hawass (right) is a famous Egyptologist. He is in charge of all ancient Egyptian excavations and structures. Dr. Hawass is a pyramid expert. He states that the Giza pyramids were once covered with gleaming white limestone. Dr. Hawass says, "These pyramids were monuments and tombs for the pharaohs and queens. The inside walls were painted with scenes. They often showed people carrying gifts for the pharaoh.

"When the pharaoh died, the body was placed on a wooden barge. The barge was towed along a canal to the foot of the pyramids.

Dr. Hawass supervised the renovation of the Great Sphinx at Giza. The Sphinx has guarded the pyramids for more than 4,000 years.

Then the barge was pulled into the pyramid. A procession of priests and priestesses carried offerings to be sealed in the burial chamber."

Dr. Hawass says, "When I hold an ancient find, it is like cradling a baby in my arms. When I first saw King Tutankhamen's face unwrapped, I cried. I love my work with the dead."

During the 1800s and early 1900s, many ancient Egyptian artifacts left Egypt. They went to museums around the world. For instance, the bust of Queen Nefertiti is held in the Egyptian Museum in Berlin, Germany. Many Egyptian artifacts also went to private collections.

Today, it is illegal to remove ancient artifacts from Egypt. In fact, Egyptologist Dr. Zahi Hawass would like to see all ancient Egyptian artifacts returned to Egypt.

WHAT DO YOU THINK?

Should museums around the world return ancient Egyptian artifacts to the Egyptian government?

PRO

I think many artifacts were taken out of Egypt illegally in the past. They should be returned to Egypt. That is where they belong. They are an important part of Egypt's culture and history.

Rosetta Stone, British Museum,
London, England

In July 2003, the Egyptian government asked the British Museum for a loan of the Rosetta Stone. This important artifact was found in Egypt in 1799. It later went to England. It provided the key to the lost language of ancient Egypt.

However, museums around the world are reluctant to lend or return artifacts. They believe that such items are what attract so many visitors to their museums.

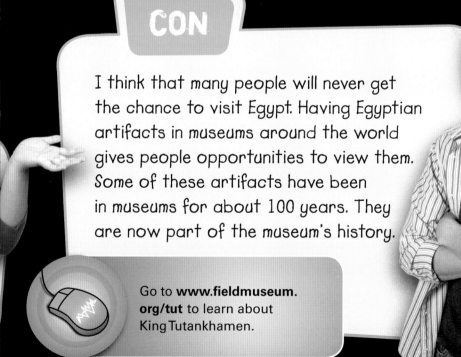

CON

I think that many people will never get the chance to visit Egypt. Having Egyptian artifacts in museums around the world gives people opportunities to view them. Some of these artifacts have been in museums for about 100 years. They are now part of the museum's history.

Go to **www.fieldmuseum. org/tut** to learn about King Tutankhamen.

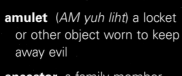

amulet (*AM yuh liht*) a locket or other object worn to keep away evil

ancestor a family member who died long ago

ancient (*AYN shunt*) very old or from long ago

barge a flat-bottomed boat used for transporting goods on waterways

canal (*kuh NAL*) a channel dug across land to connect bodies of water

canopic jar a jar used in ancient Egyptian times that held a dead person's vital organs

chariot (*CHA ree uht*) a small, two-wheeled vehicle, pulled by a horse, used in ancient Egyptian times

CT scan a kind of X-ray that shows a cross-sectional image of a person's body

dimension the length, width, or height of a shape or an object

emotion a strong feeling, such as happiness, love, or anger

inscribe (*in SKRIBE*) to carve letters into a surface, such as stone

polio (*POH lee oh*) a disease that affects the brain and spinal cord

portrait an artistic likeness of a person

pyramid (*PIHR uh mid*) a massive monument with a square base and four triangular walls, with inner burial chambers

quarry (*KWOR ee*) a place where stone is dug, cut, or blasted out of the ground

radiologist (*ray dee OL uh jist*) a person who takes X-rays

smallpox (*SMAWL poks*) a serious disease that causes chills, high fever, and a rash

suspect (*SUSS pekt*) a person who is believed to be responsible for a crime or an accident

syndrome (*SIN drohm*) a group of symptoms that occur together

tomb (*TOOM*) a small building where a dead person is buried